Yellow Umbrella Books are published by Capstone Press
151 Good Counsel Drive, P.O. Box 669, Mankato, Minnesota 56002
http://www.capstone-press.com

Library of Congress Cataloging-in-Publication Data
Schaefer, Lola M., 1950–
   Models/by Lola Schaefer.
   p. cm.
   Includes index.
   ISBN 0-7368-0731-4
   1. Models and modelmaking—Juvenile literature. [1. Models and modelmaking.] I. Title.
TT154.S345   2001
745.5928—dc21   00-036476

   Summary: Explains what a model is and describes various types of models and
their functions.

Editorial Credits:
Susan Evento, Managing Editor/Product Development; Elizabeth Jaffe, Senior Editor;
   Sydney Wright and Charles Hunt, Designers; Kimberly Danger and Heidi Schoof,
   Photo Researchers

Photo Credits:
Cover: Photo Network/Tom McCarthy; Title Page: Scott Campbell; Page 2: Index Stock
Imagery; Page 3: Josef Beck/FPG International LLC; Page 4: International Stock/George
Ancona (left), International Stock/Hilary Wilkes (right); Page 5: Unicorn Stock Photos/Tom
McCarthy (left), Visuals Unlimited/Mark Gibson (right); Page 6: International Stock/Mark
Gibson; Page 7: Visuals Unlimited/Joe McDonald (right); Page 8: Unicorn Stock Photos/Dennis
Thompson (top), Unicorn Stock Photos/Arni Katz (bottom); Page 9: Photophile/Mark Gibson
(top), Unicorn Stock Photos/Joe Sohms (bottom right); Page 10: Leslie O'Shaughnessy (left),
Index Stock Imagery (right); Page 11: Visuals Unlimited/Mark Gibson; Page 12: Visuals
Unlimited/Gary Carter; Page 13: Index Stock Imagery; Page 14: Index Stock Imagery (left),
Photo Network/Larry Dunmir (right); Page 15: Ed Degginger (left), Norbert Wu (right);
Page 16: Unicorn Stock Photos/Jeff Greenberg

1 2 3 4 5 6 06 05 04 03 02 01

Models

By Lola Schaefer

Consulting Editor: Gail Saunders-Smith, Ph.D.
Consultants: Claudine Jellison and
Patricia Williams, Reading Recovery Teachers
Content Consultant: Jaleh Daie, Ph. D.,
President, Women in Science and Technology Alliance,
Professor, University of Wisconsin

Yellow Umbrella Books

an imprint of Capstone Press
Mankato, Minnesota

People make models.
Models look like real objects.
Models help people learn
about real objects.

Some models are smaller
than the real object.
This model of buildings
is smaller than real buildings.

Some models are larger
than the real object.
This model of a mouth
is bigger than a real mouth.

Some models are the same size as the real thing.

It is easier to study
models of elephants
than it is to study
real elephants.

This is a model of the real car.

This is the real car.

How are the cars the same?
How are the cars different?

A globe
is a model
of Earth.
We can see all lands and
bodies of water on a globe.

Some models let us see what the inside of things look like.

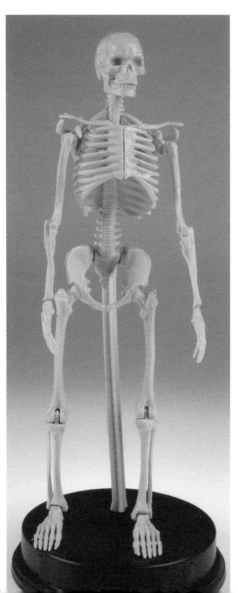

These models show what the inside of your body looks like.

You use the inside
of your body
when you work and play.

This dollhouse shows
what the inside and outside
of a real house can look like.

How is this real house
different from a dollhouse?

Some models look and move
like the real thing.
Wind moves real and model
sailboats across the water.

This fish tank is a model
of a real body of water
where fish live. It has rocks,
plants, and water.

You can make models too.

What can you learn
from making a model?

Words to Know/Index

building—a structure with walls and a roof; page 4

different—not the same; pages 8, 13

dollhouse—a small home built for toys; pages 12, 13

Earth—the planet on which we live; page 9

fish tank—a glass container filled with water in which fish can live; page 15

globe—a round model of Earth; page 9

object—something that can be seen and touched; pages 2, 4, 5

sailboat—a craft with a large sheet of strong cloth; sailboats move on water when the wind blows; page 14

same—alike; pages 6, 8

Word Count: 230
Early-Intervention Levels: 9–12